# WEATHERING
# LIFE'S
# STORMS

# WEATHERING
# LIFE'S
# STORMS

*Equipping Yourself to Face the Challenges*

TABITHA HENTON LAMB

# CONTENTS

# INTRODUCTION

The purpose of this book is to bring hope and encouragement during these times of uncertainty when we are all going through great loss and suffering. The message is to keep fighting the good fight of faith and to not give up. All of us will face the storms of life through sickness, the loss of a loved one, some financial crisis, and it is our earnest prayer for that storm to pass. I agree with that prayer. But I also pray for the revelation that the storm is there for a purpose and there is greater good in the process if we cooperate with the Spirit of God. We must remember during those times that God is equipping us for greater things than we can imagine.

I have faced many storms and struggled, not only with the storm itself but with why the storm was allowed…until the revelation came to me that God was at work in me in the process.

This book prepares us for storms, whether caused by us, by others or by things we are asked to suffer for Christ. We are to face each storm with courage and faith with the assurance that God will never forsake us. This is why the apostle James admonished us to count it all joy when we face trials (James 1:2).

Naturally you ask: "How can I come to a posture of heart and mind to be joyful in the midst of pain?" "How can suffering be beneficial?" "Am I being punished?" "How am I to prepare myself for storms?" These are important questions that will be addressed in this book, so we have a clear understanding of the purpose of storms and where God wants to bring us.

Let's begin by following the brave ones that went before us and experienced their own storms. Paul went through all kinds of storms in life from actual shipwreck, to being beaten and thrown into a Roman prison to suffering deprivation, including rejection by his own people. Jeremiah was ridiculed for preaching repentance, and landed in prison, but he continued to warn people as instructed by God. Job lost his children and all his possessions as well as his health in one blow; but he did not curse God. Instead, he sought the Lord to know why.

David found himself living in and out of caves, forced to

go into hiding because Saul was looking to kill him. Out of hatred for him, Saul took the daughter he had given David in marriage and gave her to another man. In all of this, David did not give up on God but cried out to Him. A good portion of the psalms was written by him during his times of sorrow. All these heroes of faith were finally vindicated and received their reward.

Then there was Joseph, who was hated by his brothers – though this was often instigated by his pride. He was thrown into a pit, sold into slavery, and ended up in prison. In spite of all the hardships, he trusted the plan of God for his life, and eventually became the second most important person after Pharaoh in Egypt.

Jesus endured the greatest suffering of any human on earth. Yet He did not turn away from His Father but clung to Him. He came to a place where nothing mattered but the Will of God, which had to be accomplished at all costs, even if it meant an end to His life.

Dear reader, if you are going through trials, take heart, for God has a word for you through this exposition.

In this book I want to address several things, so we have a vivid idea of suffering. First, we will look at the real enemy and his modus operandi. We will then look at the weapons of our warfare and how we must stand in the evil day.

Things are not going to get easier, in these turbulent times, my friend, and we are better suited if we brace ourselves for perilous times.

However, we have a hope and a guide in Christ when we learn to work with the weapons that God has given us. They are there to protect us and enable us to take the offensive against the enemy. When we follow these guidelines, we will learn to be strong and resilient in our storms of life.

CHAPTER
1

# KNOW YOUR ENEMY

T he first thing we must be aware of is that this is a
battle between good and evil. For those of us on
the Lord's side, His enemies have joined forces
against us as an indirect assault on Him. In order for us to
make it through the attack with no damage, we must not
fall into his trap of putting the blame on the human parties
who appear to have wronged us. No, this is the wrong battleground. If we fight it here, our fighting strategy will be
counterproductive. The purpose is better served by knowing
our real enemy. This battle called life is a spiritual battle, with
spiritual enemies, for spiritual purposes.

The apostle Paul defines this battleground in
the book of Ephesians.

*For we wrestle not against flesh and blood, but
against principalities, against powers, against the
rulers of the darkness of this world, against spiritual wickedness in high places* (Ephesians 6:12).

What does it mean to wrestle?

It is a picture of the Saints on earth engaging in close
combat with Spirit rebels who are against God. We are not
wrestling with human opponents, or even against our corrupt nature. No, we are wrestling with diabolical entities,
who are immensely stronger, more intelligent, and more
cunning than we are. Make no mistake; the enemy is Satan
and his cohorts. This is a subtle enemy with multitudinous
ways of beguiling a soul that is not firmly rooted on the
word. Satan is described as a serpent because his nature is
subtle: he knows the weaknesses of man and disguises himself as a friend. Paul referred to him as an "angel of light" (1
Corinthians 11:14). He is a master of the art of distraction,
deception, attraction and seduction.

Satan controls this world through a hierarchy of fallen
angels and demon spirits with different spheres of authority,
within a well-organized chain of command. No wonder
Jesus referred to him as "the ruler of the world" (John 14:30)!
His kingdom is governed by principalities, powers, and rulers, spiritual wickedness in high places or wicked spirits. All

are numerous, skillful and relentless in their attack on the children of God.

From Paul's description, we can identify four levels of his fiendish authority:

- Principalities – chief rulers, the highest rank in Satan's kingdom
- Authorities – whose power is derived from the chief rulers and whose will they execute
- World rulers – spirit rulers of darkness who control nations or regions
- Spiritual wickedness – wicked spirits of Satan who control humans and nations

How does the enemy infiltrate and control people, rulers and nations?

The main entry point is the mind. This is where the real battleground is. If he can defeat you in your thought life, the battle is already won. His strategy is lying. How does he do this? Through planting seeds of deception, and strongholds of unbelief that question God's promises, to germinate in your mind. For instance, **he led Eve to question the integrity of God**, thereby enabling a stronghold of doubt and unbelief – even suspicion of God and His word – to be formed in her mind. From there, with her mind now within

3

his sphere of control, he was then able to move in and tempt her to eat from the tree of the knowledge of good and evil.

Let's look closer at strongholds.

Strongholds are described by Paul in 2 Corinthians 10:3-6.

> *For though we walk in the flesh, we do not war after the flesh: (For the weapons of our warfare are not carnal, but mighty through God to the pulling down of strong holds;) Casting down imaginations, and every high thing that exalteth itself against the knowledge of God, and bringing into captivity every thought to the obedience of Christ; And having in a readiness to revenge all disobedience, when your obedience is fulfilled.*

Strongholds are areas of resistance to God's word in the hearts and minds of those whom Satan has manipulated and deceived, just as he did Eve. However, we are not powerless. Using the weapons provided to us by God, we can demolish mental arguments, and capture thoughts in order to empower ourselves and others to continue in obedience to Christ. These weapons are the only ones that are powerful enough to defeat our true enemy. If human tactics and responses are what you avail yourself of as your defense system, then your weapons are ineffective. The enemy would have you believe that you are battling flesh and blood. This method is one of his best ploys to disguise himself – but we are not ignorant of his wiles.

Let's break down 2 Corinthians 10:3-6 step by step.

> *For though we walk in the flesh, we do not war after the flesh* (verse 3).

Here "the flesh" implies **our flawed belief systems and human thought processes, as well as our carnal habits.** All of these create vulnerabilities for Satan to invade. For though we walk in the flesh and live in a physical body, we are to avoid the flawed belief systems, (ignorance of the truth of His word) human thought processes (human mind with its reasonings) carnal habits, (fleshly deeds that prohibit the ability to be led by His Spirit) as our fighting strategy in this spiritual battle.

> *For the weapons of our warfare are not carnal, but mighty through God to the pulling down of strong holds* (verse 4).

The weapons we use are mighty and powerful because they are instituted by God for our use. They are designed specifically for the attacks of our enemies. Only God knows the true composition of this enemy, so we must trust in what He provides to defeat them.

With Strongholds this tactic attempts to make the word of God null and void in our minds. So we use our weapons for the pulling down of these strongholds, to destroy the reasoning that strives to make the word of God of no effect. We are to war against these forces until we pull them down totally, and put to flight all mental intrusion and evil power. How do we do this?

> *Casting down imaginations, and every high thing that exalteth itself against the knowledge of God ...* (verse 5).

We are to cast down all vain imaginations, and demolish all theories, speculations, belief systems, philosophies – any thoughts that are contrary to the true intelligence of God, His word, His integrity and character.

Let's identify the strategies used by Satan to build strongholds in our minds. He uses our ignorance, prejudice, lusts of all kinds, and hidden motives as a landing point to invade the mind. He endeavors to keep us from faith and therefore rob us of our desire and need of allegiance to God and obedience to His Word. His ultimate aim is to take us as his possession and to assume ownership of us just like the owner of a title deed.

We are to counter that move by bringing all thoughts held captive by him back to Jesus. We gather all unchecked thoughts and bring them under subjection to the obedience of Christ.

> *...and bringing into captivity every thought to*
> *the obedience of Christ* (verse 5).

How do I make my thoughts obedient to Christ?

By using the Word of God. The word of God is our weapon and we must use it as our reference in all given matters. If it's a thought to make you reject anything in God's word, for example, that God has forgotten about you, don't accept it – cast it out immediately. If it's a don't-forgive kind of a thought, then remind yourself what the bible says about forgiveness and apply it in your situation. We must forgive if we want His forgiveness.

If it is a thought to provoke worry or anxiety concerning finances or employment, remind yourself of what the Word indicates about these kinds of thoughts, feelings, and emotions? We are instructed to be anxious for nothing. Jesus said take no thought of what you shall eat or what you shall wear, for your Heavenly Father knows what you have need of even before you ask Him. Accept this as the truth, and reject any other.

If the thought concerns your health or that of a loved one – we know the stripes of Jesus paid for our healing and recovery. Pray and meditate on scriptures for healing.

If you struggle with thoughts of low self-esteem or acceptance, remember you are fearfully and wonderfully made, and this your soul has to know very well. Marvelous are His works, and you are one of His works.

If the thoughts concern emotions – pain, sadness, hurt pain or shame – guard your heart and ask the Lord to intervene in your situation. Of course, it is natural to grieve when something bad happens. But do not allow grieving to settle in your heart for too long. The devil will continue his attempts to weigh you down with such thoughts to damage your soul, so quickly encourage yourself by praying and meditating on His word. We must guard our hearts with all diligence for out of it are the issues of life.

Thoughts become cares only when we accept them and take ownership of them. When we agree with the thought and say, "Thought, you know what? You're right; this is what I think, what I feel and what I see," then we give it power to become real to us. Prior to this, it was only a suggestive thought – no more – and we have every right to reject it.

Our dependency is completely upon God. This is our resolve to cast our existing and future cares on Him, for He cares for us.

Let's look at a man who worried a lot – Job. Job was a righteous man before God and in no way was to blame for the severe trials that came upon him. This was solely the work of Satan. All the same, Job was constantly anxious that his sons and daughters might sin, and so he offered sacrifices to placate God in case they offended Him. The devil knew this, and when the time came to afflict the man, he knew his places of vulnerability and where exactly to strike. To Job what happened was a real enactment of his fears: *"For the thing I greatly feared has come upon me, And what I dreaded has happened to me"* (Job 3:25).

Therefore, when thoughts of doubt or fear come to you, what does the Word of God say concerning these? **"Perfect love casts out all fear"** (1 John 4:18), so meditate on scriptures that remind you of the love of God. Once you come to know, to understand and to believe in His nature, then you are empowered to reject fear and doubt.

The Word of God has already been proven, tried and tested. It is what spoke time and the world we now live in into existence – not one of us wakes up in the morning hoping the earth is still spinning on its axis. If we can exercise this kind of faith in what He has created, why not transfer that same faith over to Him?

So when you take your thoughts captive, you come to a resolve to cherish the things of God, His Word and His revelation of Himself to you. It is only when you get to know a person that you can come to love them. So it is with God. If we can fall in love with someone based on the persona they present, then we can also come to fall deeply in love with God based on His abundantly clear revelation of Himself, His goodness and His reckless love toward us. You will fall head over heels in love with Him as you discover the true lover of your soul. Only He can satisfy your deep longing for acceptance and fellowship, and fill you completely from the inside out.

Then you will come to learn of His ways and become secure, knowing there is no fault in Him. Your finite mind will rest easy as you begin to believe the thoughts He has for you, thoughts of good and not of evil to bring you to an expected end (Jeremiah 29:11). What is this end? For us it is true sonship.

And so, as we pull back each thought that is contrary to His word, we gain ground for Christ to rule our minds.

We know now that our enemies are not people but demonic powers who want to take possession of our mind through setting up strongholds which make us deny the trustworthiness of God. They want to rob us of true sonship in that we relinquish our authority and power. They want to keep us from experiencing all of the benefits made available to us as His children.

The next thing we will do is discuss the weapons of our warfare in detail so we can put on the armor of God.

# PUT ON YOUR ARMOR

N ow that we know who our enemy is and what his strategy is, the next question is: how do we fight this battle?

The detailed answer comes from Ephesians 6:10-18, the armor God gives us. Just as the battle is in the mind as we learned in 2 Corinthians 10:3-6, so too are our weapons formed in the mind.

Now, before we put on this armor, we must determine to fortify our mind with the strength and power of the Lord, not our own. In this effort we are admonished to,

*...be strong in the Lord, and in the power of his might* (Ephesians 6:10).

The first command is to be strong. We must take our strength from the Lord because in the natural we lack the required strength and easily get weary. We will certainly not win this battle in our own strength because the enemy is shrewder and a lot more experienced than us. While we do not want to admit our lack of courage for fear of being called a coward, to God our weakness is the place of His power. We must come to rely totally upon God and what His power will provide.

So we are charged to be strong with the resolve of a soldier:

- in the performance of our duties (service)
- in undergoing difficulty or unpleasantness (hardship)
- in the act of fighting in violence, conflict or battle (fighting)

Now let's study Ephesians 6:11-18:

*Put on the whole armour of God, that ye may be able to stand against the wiles of the devil. Wherefore take unto you the whole armour of God, that ye may be able to withstand in the evil*

*day, and having done all, to stand. Stand there-*
*fore, having your loins girt about with truth,*
*and having on the breastplate of righteousness;*
*And your feet shod with the preparation of the*
*gospel of peace; Above all, taking the shield of*
*faith, wherewith ye shall be able to quench all*
*the fiery darts of the wicked. And take the helmet*
*of salvation, and the sword of the Spirit, which is*
*the word of God: Praying always with all prayer*
*and supplication in the Spirit, and watching*
*thereunto with all perseverance and supplication*
*for all saints.*

Verse 11 tells us to put on the whole armor of God, so that we may be able to stand against the wiles of the devil. In essence, God is commanding us to anticipate and to prepare for the enemy's tactics. He will always prey on our weaknesses. But God is saying, "Now I will reveal to you the weapons provided by Me to overpower the enemy. They constitute the Armor of God which I designed and apportioned as Spiritual Armor for you. Make use of all the tools for defending him, so he backs off."

Our armor consists of six strategic weapons worn by a Roman soldier ready for battle:

1. The belt of truth

   *Stand therefore, having your loins girt about with truth ...* (Ephesians 6:14)

The belt of a Roman soldier consisted of a heavy leather and metal band, which held the soldier's sword and other weapons. The belt of truth of the spiritual armor holds the sword of the Spirit, linking truth with the Word of God.

Just as the belt clings to our waist, the belt of truth must cling to our inner man. With the belt holding us together, we walk in the truth of God's word within ourselves. Girding our waists with truth means we are to actively lay hold of the truth, especially to guard our inward parts against the lies and deceptions of the enemy. Without the truth upholding us, we can easily be *"tossed to and fro, and carried about with every wind of doctrine, by the sleight of men, and cunning craftiness, whereby they lie in wait to deceive..."* (Ephesians 4:14).

As the belt of truth fastens the sword of the Spirit, without it we cannot use the sword of the word accurately and will fall into error.

2. The breastplate of righteousness

   *...and having on the breastplate of righteousness...* (verse 14)

The breastplate is the righteousness of Christ imputed to us when we ask for forgiveness, and invite Him into our lives. It protects us against Satan's attacks on our vital parts. If we exercise our own righteousness, it will make us self-righteous and prideful. But when we put on Christ's righteousness, it makes us pleasing to God and therefore gives us access to Him.

Our own self-righteousness also makes us feel superior and condescending towards others. It will turn us against those who have wronged us and cause us to harbor unforgiveness. Oftentimes, the enemy will use the very ones who are closest to us to turn against us, especially if there are any fractures in the relationship. He will exploit any human weaknesses to aggravate tensions. How are we to respond when under attack from friends, associates, or family members without reason?

It's only through Christ's righteousness imputed to us that we have the grace to forgive such people just as Jesus did without malice. Look at how He responded to Judas when betrayed by him. In the same way, He forgave all of His enemies unconditionally, not charging any of their actions to them. "Father, forgive them, for they know not what they are doing," was His cry from the cross. "This may look like their hand but the blows are served from the kingdom of darkness.

They don't even realize they are being driven, deceived and used by Satan."

We, too, must forgive all who have wronged us as we seek to order things properly in our life. We are to pray for those who hurt us, and do good to those who despitefully use us. We must bless those who curse us as it safeguards our heart. And, just as the enemy has used each of us at some point to cause hurt or harm to someone else, we need to ask for forgiveness when we hurt others. We must afford others the same grace we give ourselves.

> *For if ye forgive men their trespasses, your heav-*
> *enly Father will also forgive you: But if ye forgive*
> *not men their trespasses, neither will your Father*
> *forgive your trespasses* (Matthew 6:14-15).

When we put on the breastplate of righteousness, we can come boldly to the Father and ask for His grace and mercy. Yes, we are imperfect and we all have sinned. But we can come to Him confident that when He sees us, He sees the righteousness of His Son covering us.

Ah, you may think, but my sins are too many for God to forgive. Remember the second thief who hung on the cross beside Jesus? He truly repented of his sins and made this last-minute appeal to the Savior of the world.

*Lord, remember me when thou comest into thy
kingdom* (Luke 23:42).

Did Jesus turn him away because of his high crimes? No
hear what Jesus says:

*Verily I say unto thee, Today shalt thou be with
me in paradise* (Luke 23:43).

Jesus is on the way to death and yet you see the compassionate heart of God bleeding in Him as the blood flowed
out of His wounds. He assured the thief that he would have
eternal life with Him when he cried out, "Lord, remember me!".

3. The gospel shoes

*And your feet shod with the preparation of the
gospel of peace...* (Ephesians 6:15)

Be ready to share with others the gospel of the kingdom
of God in season and out. Share the gospel through your
testimony; show it through your conduct so that all can
recognize the Christ in you, even when you are not saying a
word. The peace that comes upon you is the peace of fulfill-
ing the command of God to share Christ to others and the
knowledge that you are in His perfect will.

It's called the gospel of peace because it brings about reconciliation between God and us, and among us. Reconciliation brings peace with God, within ourselves and with others. Strive after a peaceful and a quiet mind. Show all gentleness and long suffering to all men. Determine to hold fast to the gospel and walk; then you will have a consistent stride.

4. The shield of faith

> *Above all, taking the shield of faith, wherewith*
> *ye shall be able to quench all the fiery darts of*
> *the wicked* (verse16).

Faith is a choice. It is simply taking God at His word. It means making a decision and sticking to it at all costs not based on performance or the lack of it. Faith is the substance of that which we hope for and the evidence of it until we see it.

Faith is an active thing. It's not just in the mind but it needs to be put into action. We must walk in continuous faith and absolute trust in God. Faith is also the defense mechanism we use against Satan to quench all of his fiery darts against us. We must believe we will be victorious in all spiritual warfare. Every battle will be won by God, for it is the Lord who annihilates our enemies. The only resolve is that God will bring us out. Even if we are not sure when or how, the details are up to Him to work out. It is our focus and responsibility to remain in faith until it comes to fruition.

To illustrate faith in action, let us consider the "Heroes of Faith" in Hebrews 11. Here we read about well-known figures in the Old Testament – Noah and Enoch, Abraham and Moses and the patriarchs and prophets as well as some lesser known individuals. We would expect them all to be towering giants of faith. But, surprisingly, many of them had human flaws. These caused them to doubt and sometimes waver in their trust. But God nevertheless honored them for relying on Him in their moment of weakness, and for trusting Him nonetheless.

One of the lesser known figures listed is Barak. Barak was an army general living in the time of the fourth judge, Deborah. Let's look at Barak's story in Judges 4 and 5.

We are told that the northern tribes of Israel were constantly under attack by Jabin, king of Canaan. Jabin had a formidable army under the command of Sisera, which boasted nine hundred chariots of iron, and sophisticated weaponry.

It was at this time that Deborah had a message from God and summoned Barak.

*"Has not the LORD God of Israel commanded, 'Go and deploy troops at Mount Tabor; take with you ten thousand men*

of the sons of Naphtali and of the sons of Zebulun" (Judges 4:
6 NKJV). God promised to deliver Sisera with his chariots
and army at the River Kishon into Israel's hand (verse 7).

Now look at the way Barak answered: *"If you will go with
me, then I will go; but if you will not go with me, I will not
go!"* Coming from a general, that did not inspire confidence.

Deborah agreed to accompany him to battle (verses 8-9).

Now the fact that Barak's acceptance of the challenge
was conditional upon Deborah being present showed that
he put more trust in Deborah's relationship with God than
his. He needed Deborah at the scene of battle to inspire and
assure him of the certain help of Almighty God, so his faith
lay in Deborah's influence with God rather than in his own.

Nevertheless, once Barak decided to go out, he and all
the armies who went displayed real courage and trust in God
in the battle. They had essentially no weapons to match such
a superior force. What was worse was that God increased
the odds against them when He commanded them to fight
on the river plain, a move to the advantage of the chariots
over the men on foot. Engaging with such an army in such
a battleground was a tremendous act of faith by Barak.

But God turned the tide. He sent down torrential rains
bringing a flash flood to the plain. The iron chariots were
helpless in the mud and tried to escape (Judges 5:21). *"But*

*Barak pursued the chariots and the army as far as Harosheth Hagoyim, and all the army of Sisera fell by the edge of the sword; not a man was left"* (Judges 4:16).

Interestingly, it is Barak not Deborah who is mentioned among the heroes of faith (Hebrews 11:32). Each one of those on the list was a man or woman of faith, yet many had notable areas of failure in their life. Still, Hebrews 11 commends their faith. This shows that weak faith is acceptable to God as a starting point, and you don't have to be perfect to make it into God's list of heroes. This is so encouraging for many of us who are hesitant at first. But when we bring these weaknesses before God, He will show Himself strong in the battle we are called to fight.

5. The helmet of salvation

*And take the helmet of salvation* …(Ephesians 6:17)

The helmet is there to protect the head, and therefore our thought life, from wrong and damaging thoughts. We are what we eat and what we feed our minds we become, for as a man thinks in his heart so is he. We must stand in confident assurance that we belong to Him, not by our own make-up but by His design. We must learn to see ourselves the way God sees us. Do we truly believe we are children of God? If we do, this will determine how we weather the storms of life and how we come out of them.

We heard about the arguments the enemy uses to ensnare our minds in 2 Corinthians 10:5-6. One of the devil's favorite ways of attacking our mind is through fear. Fear is a spirit and, if God has not given us the spirit of fear, then we know where it came from.

We must understand that fear leaves open doors, giving the enemy access to all that belongs to us to wreak havoc in our lives. We must get the fear out of our mind and come to understand the truth about God and His love for us. We must put on this truth to ensure that our belief system is governed only by what God's word has to say about His nature and love for us.

You don't have to fear any of the attacks against you; they are powerful only if you submit to them by giving yourself over to them. Once you are aware of the devil's fear tactics to gain advantage over you, you will guard your mind. The love of God is the primary weapon we are to use against fear.

Take inventory and find out what you hold true about God. What do you truly believe about His love for you? His plans for your life? His thoughts concerning you? Then replace each untruth with the truth of His word. This is the weapon that is required when you see attacks of fear, so be ready to pull the appropriate word from your arsenal by meditating and continually walking and standing in truth.

God knows the truth about our weaknesses and doesn't condemn us. For this reason, He has committed Himself and His love more passionately to us. Don't be alarmed by the tactics of the enemy to entrap you in fear. Stand in faith lavished by the love of God.

6. The sword of the Spirit

> *... and the sword of the Spirit, which is the word of God......* (Ephesians 6:17)

Hebrews 4:12 tells us that the word of God is living and active, and sharper than any two-edged sword to the extent that it can divide soul from spirit, and discern the thoughts and intentions of the heart.

This word can distinguish between the thoughts, feelings and emotions that belong to the soul and those that belong to the spirit, for the spirit can also experience strong emotions and groan in pain. All emotions have a strong pull on us but the word helps us to discern whether they are of God or from ourselves, and keep us in check.

How is the sword put into operation? Mainly through the words we speak. Revelation 19:11-21 gives us a vivid picture of the victorious Christ, whose name is The Word, descending from heaven on a white horse with His armies. Now note: *"And out of **his mouth** goeth a sharp sword, that with it he should smite the nations ..."* (verse15, emphasis added). Not His hand but His mouth. How does the sword go out of His mouth? Through His words. Just as God created the heavens and earth by the words of His mouth, so too will Jesus release the word of judgment against rebellious nations.

While on earth Jesus Himself told us that His words *"they* are spirit, and *they* are life" (John 6:63) and, by implication, our words are spirit and life too.

Remember how Ezekiel was commanded to speak to the dry bones in the valley until they formed into human beings, and then speak to the four winds to breathe into them that they might live (Ezekiel 37:1-10)? Remember how Moses too was commanded to speak to the rock and it would pour out water (Numbers 20:7-8)?

Therefore we have the power based on the word of God to speak life over dead situations, over impossible ones, over deteriorating health, relationships or finances, and revive them. When the enemy comes against us, we are to use the Word of God having made preparation for this day to come. What are the weaknesses or common areas of attack in your life? Find scriptures that are applicable to those areas and meditate on them diligently until they are committed to memory. When he comes, these are the words you will use against him in authority and faith. Refuse all of his onslaughts and accept nothing except what the Word has to say regarding your situation. If we resist him like we really mean it, he has no choice but to flee. However we must do our part for this to happen. So we stand in faith on the word of God and we use it with Authority.

Equally, we have the power to release words of destruction over all the power of the enemy, to dismantle his plans and every one of his assignments against the people of God. Such is the power of the spoken word released according to God's purposes. This is the sword of the Spirit.

One last point. While each of the six weapons has its specific function, they all work together, supporting and reinforcing one another. This means you must put on the *full* armor of God and leave nothing missing. Imagine going into battle without the helmet of salvation and being mentally bombarded by the negative thoughts of the enemy so that even the shield of faith cannot quench them. Imagine not putting on the breastplate of righteousness with the shoes of the gospel of peace so that our sharing is based on our own self-righteousness, and puts people off.

In the next chapter we will discuss some more powerful weapons which are not so obvious to Satan. Stay tuned!

# OUR INVISIBLE WEAPONS

The enemy is aware of our spiritual armor but the invisible weapons in our arsenal are not so obvious. These are the weapons of prayer and supplication, together with perseverance.

> *Praying always with all prayer and supplication in the Spirit, and watching thereunto with all perseverance and supplication for all saints ...* (Ephesians 6:18)

We can add to this the weapon of love.

# PRAYER AND SUPPLICATION

Although prayer is not a classified part of the armor, it is a crucial part of the fight. We are to pray with all of the components of prayer: confessions of sins, petitions for mercy, thanksgiving for favors received, praying in the Spirit. Prayer helps to buckle on all of the other parts of the Christian armor. We must join in prayer to protect all of our pieces of armor from our spiritual enemies. Jesus taught us to always to pray, and not faint... (Luke 18:1)

When Paul urges us to pray with *all* supplication, I believe it includes passionate prayer – as if our life depended on it. Here I want to highlight the prayer Paul describes in Romans 8:28. *"And we know that all things work together for good to them that love God, to them who are the called according to his purpose."* We see this in the story of Lazarus. Let's look at John 11:

> *When Jesus therefore saw her [Mary's] weeping, and the Jews also weeping which came with her, he groaned in the spirit, and was troubled. And said, Where have ye laid him? They said unto him, Lord, come and see. Jesus wept. Then said the Jews, Behold how he loved him! And some of them said, Could not this man, which opened*

30

*the eyes of the blind, have caused that even this man should not have died?"*

*Jesus therefore again groaning in himself cometh to the grave. It was a cave, and a stone lay upon it. Jesus said, Take ye away the stone.*

*Martha, the sister of him that was dead, saith unto him, Lord, by this time he stinketh: for he hath been dead four days.*

*Jesus saith unto her, Said I not unto thee, that, if thou wouldest believe, thou shouldest see the glory of God?*

*Then they took away the stone from the place where the dead was laid. And Jesus lifted up his eyes, and said, Father, I thank thee that thou hast heard me. And I knew that thou hearest me always: but because of the people which stand by I said it, that they may believe that thou hast sent me. And when he thus had spoken, he cried with a loud voice, Lazarus, come forth.*

*And he that was dead came forth, bound hand and foot with graveclothes: and his face was*

*bound about with a napkin. Jesus saith unto*
*them, Loose him, and let him go. Then many of*
*the Jews which came to Mary, and had seen the*
*things which Jesus did, believed on him* (John
11:41-45, emphasis added).

Jesus is saying, "I'm not praying for Myself but for those
around Me that they may believe that the Father has sent
Me." Then He cries out with a loud voice, "Lazarus I know
that death is holding you but I command you to come forth."
Note that He did not speak to the spirit of death but He
directed His command purposefully at Lazarus. "You see,
Lazarus, death cannot hold you any time beyond what My
Father has allowed, and time has reached its limit in this
matter. My Father has power over that which is holding you
'captive to death.' So I command you to come forth out of
this state that can no longer hold you. It was allowed only
that the Glory of God might be revealed and since His Glory
is tied in your resurrection, Lazarus, My friend, the one I
love, come forth, that the Glory of God might be revealed!"

I pray we get this truth: what happened to Lazarus had
nothing to do with him. However, by the foreknowledge of
God, death was allowed to claim his body – but only for a
season – but even in this state there was an end.

People of God, we must come to a place of absolute trust

in the Sovereignty of our God. Death had no power over Lazarus against the Will of God. As a matter of fact, Jesus considered it only a state of "sleep." What we deem death and tragic, He sees only as a passing thing. Wow! We must grasp this truth. We must hold on to it, even when things die and come to a state of decay in our lives and in the lives of those, we hold dear. We must make a firm decision to pray to God in faith and to trust Him in spite of all that has happened. God knows what He is doing.

The end resolve of all you encounter must be to secure the Glory of God by any means necessary. Our prayer must be "Secure Your Glory in my life, Lord! This assures me that You must and will come through for me. Your Glory is vested in me. Do all that is required. I give you permission to secure it."

> *...and watching thereunto with all persever-*
> *ance ...*(verse 18)

To persevere in hardship, we cannot trust our flesh-life. We must abandon it at any cost. We must trust the path laid out for us by God and know He will keep us. For He knows the journey we must take. The flesh-life must be crucified together with all of its passions and lusts. He alone knows what is required to produce true obedience. In this, trust you are tucked away in Him; remain snug there and do not come out of this place of safety.

We will say more about perseverance in the next chapter. For now, I want to introduce one more invisible weapon.

## THE WEAPON OF LOVE

How often is it that we've asked, "God, why is it so hard for me to walk in Your unconditional love?"

And He replies, "Because your love is conditional just like the love the world gives. It is love as long as there is an absence of the real facts or a denial of them. My love is all inclusive to contain all of the facts and the truth of what happens. My love allows you to love what the world deems unlovable.

"The kind of love I want to display upon you is an offense to you. Are you offended by My love? Blessed is the man who is not offended in Me (Matthew 11:6). I want to heal you from the inside out, showing My goodness towards you. But because you have a distorted notion of goodness, you cannot comprehend or grasp the value of My love. You cannot handle the true lover of your soul."

The perfect love of God shatters all fear (1 John 4:18).

Fear is: False Evidence Appearing Real. It has to do with torment and punishment.

Do not have any false expectations of the ones you love in order for you to walk in unconditional love. Expect to be successful, but at the same time identify the things that can encroach upon the expression of this kind of love.

What boundaries are hindering our love walk with others? What is the ultimate in our minds when it comes to administering unconditional love? Do you have that "I will love you…" stipulation "as long as you do not… cheat on, hurt me, disappoint me, lie to me, steal from me, deceive me, break my heart or abandon me?"

Jesus is our perfect display of love – He came not so much to be loved or to receive love as to give Himself as a love offering.

Jesus summed up all the ten commandments under only two: love the Lord your God with all your heart, and love your neighbor as you love yourself. All the law and the prophets hang on these two commandments (Matthew 22:36-40).

Replace anger with grace immediately in your relationships. If anger is left unchecked, thoughts of hurt, anger and pain will pierce your heart and form a stronghold. We must use wisdom when we receive mistreatment from others to set a plan in motion. The ultimate thing is to pray for others when they hurt or disappoint us, so we can continue to experience and give unconditional love as the word of God commands.

Now, the human heart is incapable of unconditional love. It only knows how to love when loved according to a certain level of performance. When that falls short of expectation, the love is held back. But God loves us unconditionally regardless of how we reciprocate. And, just as He loves unconditionally, so does He put into our hearts the capacity to love Him and to love others. If He commanded us to love as such, then surely it is possible to receive it as He gives it to us.

This love is called *agape* love, That's the way God loves us and the way we should respond. As we read this passage, let's look at some of the characteristics of this unique love. These are also included in my *Enriching the Immortal Soul* book.

> *Love endures with patience and serenity, love is kind and thoughtful, and is not jealous or envious; love does not brag and is not proud or arrogant. It is not rude; it is not self-seeking; it is not provoked [nor overly sensitive and easily angered]; it does not take into account a wrong endured. It does not rejoice at injustice, but rejoices with the truth [when right and truth prevail]. Love bears all things [regardless of what*

*comes], believes all things [looking for the best in each one], hopes all things [remaining steadfast during difficult times], endures all things [without weakening]* (1 Corinthians 13:4-7 AMP).

There are nine characteristics of *agape* love:

1. Patience – love bides its time; does not demand; believes, hopes, and endures without complaint
2. Kindness – is always thoughtful and caring, seeking only the good of others
3. Generosity – gives freely, not holding back; never in competition: not envious or jealous
4. Humility – is not boastful or proud, simple with no airs; not waiting on men's praise
5. Courtesy – shows respect for others, acts with dignity; always polite; at home with all classes; never rude or discourteous; gracious
6. Unselfishness –seeks to accommodate the needs of others; does not retaliate or seek revenge
7. Good Temper – is never irritated, resentful or quick to retaliate when offended; does not hit out in passionate anger or brood over wrongs
8. Righteousness – is just; abides by God's commands; is never glad when others go wrong or are exposed; glad

to see the goodness of God in others; always eager to believe the best in others; forgiving

9. Sincerity – genuine and transparent to all regardless of social class; not a hypocrite; always honest; no hidden agenda; never imposing; knows how to be silent; full of trust; joyful, and truthful

In light of the above, let us re-evaluate our own ability to give and receive love. We must first go to the Father and receive His perfect love. Ask Him for His compassion to see and treat people the way He does. Let us cover their weaknesses the way He covers ours with the breastplate of righteousness. Let's refrain from always having to be in the right, but learn to give way to others, allowing the truth to surface through gentle reasoning.

And when those we love do us wrong, let us love them all the same. Even the world loves those who are kind to them. But it takes a special love to continue to love in darkness, to exercise love where there is hate or betrayal. Let us not love because a person is good, kind or deserving but let us love because God wants the perfect love of the Son of God to shine through us.

And let us obey what God calls us to do even when our mind would want to resist or even when it hurts. Mature love is the ability to love in word and in deed.

To extend the gift of love, we learn that the Holy Spirit has given us nine fruit. These are all meant to shape our character to make us more like Christ. Here they are:

> *But the fruit of the Spirit [the result of His presence within us] is love [unselfish concern for others], joy, [inner] peace, patience [not the ability to wait, but how we act while waiting], kindness, goodness, faithfulness, gentleness, self-control. Against such things there is no law. And those who belong to Christ Jesus have crucified the sinful nature together with its passions and appetites* (Galatians 5:22-24) AMP.

There are Nine Fruit of the Spirit and these can be divided into group of three Spirit:

The first three are for my benefit:

1. Love - Divine love - A strong, ardent tender, compassionate, devotion to the well-being of another
2. Joy - The emotional excitement, gladness, delight over blessings received for self and for others
3. Peace - The state of quietness, rest, repose, harmony, order, and security in the midst of turmoil, strife, and temptation

The second three are for the benefit of others:

4.  Longsuffering - Patient endurance; to bear long with the frailties, offenses, injuries, and provocations of others, without murmuring, repining, or resentment
5.  Gentleness - A disposition to be gentle, soft spoken, kind, even tempered, cultured and refined in character and conduct.
6.  Goodness - The state of being good, kind, virtuous, benevolent, generous, and God-like in life and conduct.

The last three are for the benefit of God and others:

7.  Faithfulness – The habit of being loyal, dependable, consistent and unwavering, and keeping to our word.
8.  Meekness - The disposition to be gentle, kind, indulgent, even balanced in tempers and passions, and patient in suffering injuries without entertaining a spirit of revenge.
9.  Temperance - Self-control, a moderation in the indulgence of the appetites and passions

Not surprisingly, the first fruit of the Holy Spirit is love, which immediately ties in with the gift of *agape* love we discussed just now. We see that this love embodies the characteristics of patience, kindness, goodness, gentleness, and self-control. In addition, among the fruit, we have *joy* and *peace*. These qualities reflect the presence of the Holy Spirit because we abide in the love of the Father and we do His will and the things that are pleasing to Him. Now note that it's "fruit" not "fruits," meaning that they all come together, so your trees should display all nine, not just one or two.

The more of the fruit we possess, the more we will show forth Christ to the world. How else will the world be won over for Him? Remember, the Holy Spirit gives us nine gifts and nine fruit. While the gifts are given as and when the Holy Spirit determines (1 Corinthians 12:11), the fruit must be cultivated by us. No one can pray over us and call down patience; no, we must earnestly seek it.

Moreover, Jesus tells us that we will be known by our fruit (Matthew 7:17), not by our gifts. This is so important because by worldly standards it's our performance that matters; but people are quietly judging our character all the time. How would you like to be remembered? As a person that excelled in intelligence, persuasion, gifts of healing and deliverance, or as a person who was loving, caring and compassionate, in whose eyes people saw Jesus?

Now let us see how love played out in this remarkable episode in the life of Jesus.

Jesus loved Lazarus, but knew by foreknowledge that God had chosen Lazarus to die. It pained Him to see those around him having to suffer from this tragedy. But He accepted it. Why? For the glory of God. Jesus showed no favorites.

Let's go back to the episode in John 11.

> *Now a certain man was sick, named Lazarus,*
> *of Bethany, the town of Mary and her sister*
> *Martha. (It was that Mary which anointed the*
> *Lord with ointment, and wiped his feet with her*
> *hair, whose brother Lazarus was sick.) Therefore*
> *his sisters sent unto him, saying, Lord, behold,*
> *he whom thou lovest is sick.*

When He heard that His dear friend was very sick, what would have been the most natural thing to do? Rush to Bethany, of course. But the narrator takes an expected turn and tells us:

> *When he had heard therefore that he was sick,*
> *he abode two days still in the same place where*
> *he was.*

42

Why the word "therefore"? Was the sickness an opportunity for something bigger. What was that something?

> *When Jesus heard that, he said, This sickness is not unto death, **but for the glory of God**, that the Son of God might be glorified thereby* (emphasis added).

So we have a hint that something miraculous was about to unfold that would bring glory to God.

> Then a few days later He told his disciples they were going to Bethany.

> *Our friend Lazarus sleepeth; but I go, that I may awake him out of sleep... Howbeit Jesus spake of his death: but they thought that he had spoken of taking of rest in sleep. Then said Jesus unto them plainly, Lazarus is dead. And I am glad for your sakes that I was not there, to the intent ye may believe; nevertheless let us go unto him.*

So here we see the secondary reason – that they may believe. The miracle was a demonstration to all of the power of God. His word says, *"My Glory will I not give to another, neither my praise to a graven image"* (Isaiah 42:8). Jesus is

43

therefore saying, "I accept even this pain if You Father deem it necessary for Your glory."

When we fully comprehend how the Glory of God is at stake in our situations and how He has to bring us out because of this, each of us will begin to form a firm resilience which declares: "I am His and He loves and cares for me dearly. I am truly His beloved. He might not do things the way I would like, but I chose to be secure in His love. I will not allow Satan to gloat in his fake glory. Not for one moment will I allow it."

Are you prepared to give up everything for His glory? That, beloved, is your ultimate invisible weapon.

Now that we have learned how to use all our overt weapons and invisible weapons, let us apply 2 Corinthians 10:6:

*And having in a readiness to revenge all disobedience, when your obedience is fulfilled.*

**Obedience is never partial or selective. God is looking for our complete obedience.**

Let's look at the way Saul obeyed the instruction by God to utterly destroy the Amalekites.

> *Now go and smite Amalek, and utterly destroy*
> *all that they have, and spare them not; but slay*
> *both man and woman, infant and suckling, ox*
> *and sheep, camel and ass.*

*And he took Agag the king of the Amalekites alive, and utterly destroyed all the people with the edge of the sword. But Saul and the people spared Agag, and the best of the sheep, and of the oxen, and of the fatlings, and the lambs, and all that was good, and would not utterly destroy them: but every thing that was vile and refuse, that they destroyed utterly.*

*Then came the word of the LORD unto Samuel, saying, It repenteth me that I have set up Saul to be king: for he is turned back from following me, and hath not performed my commandments. And it grieved Samuel; and he cried unto the LORD all night.*

*And Samuel said, Hath the LORD as great delight in burnt offerings and sacrifices, as in obeying the voice of the LORD? Behold, to obey is better than sacrifice, and to hearken than the fat of rams.*

***For rebellion is as the sin of witchcraft, and stubbornness is as iniquity and idolatry***. *Because thou hast rejected the word of the LORD, he hath also rejected thee from being* *king* (1 Samuel 15:3, 8-11, 22-23, emphasis added).

Look how serious it is not to completely obey God. Saul was able to reason out his selective obedience but to God it was plain disobedience and was tantamount to the sin of rebellion; this was witchcraft. For that disobedience, he lost the kingdom!

Therefore, we must be very careful with how we obey God's command. Only when we have complied with what the word of God says about putting on our armor, can we prepare to punish all disobedience. This again stresses the importance of having all our weapons intact and not having chinks in our armor which can be pierced by the enemy's darts.

Now we are equipped to punish all disobedience. Psalm 149:5-9 gives us a picture of how we can execute God's judgment on our enemies. These enemies are not of flesh and blood, not individuals or groups or communities. They are from the demonic realm. Verse 9 says: "*To execute upon them the judgment written: this honour have all his saints. Praise ye the* LORD."

So you stand based on what Jesus has taught us in Luke 10:19:

*Behold, I give unto you power to tread on serpents and scorpions, and over all the power of the enemy: and nothing shall by any means hurt you.*

Our next step is to learn how to stand in the face of adversity.

# STAND IN THE EVIL DAY

*Wherefore take unto you the whole armour of God, that ye may be able to withstand **in the evil day**, and having done all, to stand* (Ephesians 6:13, emphasis added).

These *last days* are perilous times and we need to prepare our hearts to be strong and resilient. *We are told the devil is coming upon God's people with great wrath. Revelation 12:12 says: "…the devil is come down unto you, having great wrath, because he knoweth that he hath but a short time."* Knowing he *has only a short time before Jesus comes again, he is going all out to attack the saints.*

Let us practice putting on our armor daily and confronting every attack fearlessly. In the final analysis, to stand against Satan is ultimately to stand against sin, against the evil day, or any given affliction.

So what is the evil day?

Essentially, the evil day is the day of temptation. We must be prepared for it, by being trained to wield the weapons provided to us by God to expose his schemes and to resist them. First, understand there is a distinction between a temptation and a test.

A "test," means "a piercing through in order to test the durability of a substance." It is a morally neutral word. That means whether the test is for good or bad depends on the intent of the one giving the test and the response of the one tested.

On the other hand, a "temptation" is clearly a seduction or solicitation to do what is wrong. Temptations delude and lure us into doing evil with the intention of ruining us. The act of enticing is meant "to incite" or "to instigate" by exciting hope or desire, usually to do evil. Similarly, to "seduce" is to "lead astray," and to "induce to sin" by promises or persuasions to excite the passions. Flattery often operates as an enticement to sin.

> *Let no man say when he is tempted, I am tempted of God: for God cannot be tempted with evil, neither tempteth he any man: But every man is tempted, when he is drawn away of his own lust, and enticed. Then when lust hath conceived, it bringeth forth sin: and sin, when it is finished, bringeth forth death. Do not err, my beloved brethren* (James 1:13-16).

We must recognize the pull of temptation when it comes, so we can escape from it. Lust, for example, begins with just a thought which expands into a desire. Once that desire is entertained, temptation follows, opening the door of appetite. Once appetite is aroused, lust is conceived, and gives birth to sin. When the fruit is habitual sin, the final outcome is death. So temptation comes in to entice, to seduce, to lure, by allowing what is within us to draw us away from God's righteousness.

While both a temptation and a trial are an opportunity to overcome through faith and obedience to His word, we must view temptation as a call to battle and not simply as a trial. This is the kind of a stance that will produce perseverance.

Perseverance is a decision to resist the enemy in any way so that the temptation receives its proper sentence, that is, the crucifying of the flesh.

One truth we must come to grasp is that temptations will come. They are unavoidable. Even Jesus was tempted during His fast in the wilderness and many times after, whenever the devil had opportunity. Since we understand this fact, we must be prepared for the evil day.

But know that when we withstand temptation, there is great reward.

*Blessed is the man that endureth temptation: for when he is tried, he shall receive the crown of life, which the Lord hath promised to them that love him* (James 1:12).

*Wherein ye greatly rejoice, though now for a season, if need be, ye are in heaviness through manifold temptations: That the trial of your faith, being much more precious than of gold that perisheth, though it be tried with fire, might be found unto praise and honour and glory at the appearing of Jesus Christ* (1 Peter 1:6-7).

How will I be tempted?

The enemy will seek to lure us into one of the following areas of sin. We must be watchful of them and be truthful and honest with ourselves concerning our most vulnerable points. One of the worst kinds of deception is self-deception. We can be drawn into error by our own perceptions so much so we focus more on the weaknesses of others, while choosing to overlook our own.

We must view ourselves, not through our own eyes but through the eyes of God, and what His word has to say about sinful flesh and its lusts and passions.

We can no longer afford to be ignorant of Satan's devices to manipulate us. A lack of denial by no means alters the truth. Let the Word of God stand true in us and let every man be a liar who accepts what is not the truth. Deception does not change what is true; it is only the imaginary belief of the one who chooses its path.

We begin with an understanding that all flesh is grass and no good thing resides in us, nothing at all to be desired in any part of our flesh. No matter how hard we may try, this is the be all and end all, the absolute TRUTH. We are going to take a very hard look at what we as sinful creatures are capable of doing due to the corrupt nature inherent in us all. When the day of temptation arrives, the same nature will rise up with the intent of trapping us into one or more of the seventeen works of the flesh listed in Galatians 5:19-21.

Four Sins of Lust:

1. Adultery – unlawful sexual relations between a man or a woman, single or married
2. Fornication – same as adultery besides all manner of other unlawful sexual relations
3. Uncleanness – in all forms that oppose purity, including sodomy, homosexuality, lesbianism, pederasty, bestiality, and all other sexual perversions
4. Lasciviousness – the promoting or partaking of activities that tend to produce lewd emotions; anything tending to foster sexual sin and lust. Pornography comes into this class

Two Sins of Impiety and Superstition:

5. Idolatry – image worship, including anything on which our affections are passionately set; extravagant admiration of the heart
6. Witchcraft – sorcery, the practice of dealing with evil spirits by means of charms, drugs and potions of various kinds.

Nine Sins of Temper:

7.  Hatred – bitter dislike, abhorrence, malice and ill-will towards anyone; tendency to hold grudges against or be angry at someone

8.  Variance – dissensions, discord, quarreling, debating; and disputes

9.  Emulations – envies, jealousies; striving to excel at the expense of another; seeking to surpass and outdo others; uncurbed spirit of rivalry in religion, business, society, and other fields of endeavor

10. Wrath – indignation and fierceness, turbulent passions; domestic and civil turmoil, rage; determined and lasting anger

11. Strife – contention, disputations; wrangling; strife with words; angry contentions; contest for superiority or advantage; strenuous endeavor to equal or pay back in kind the wrongs done to us

12. Seditions – divisions, popular disorder; stirring up strife in religion, government, home, or any other place

13. Heresies – holding beliefs or opinions contrary to orthodox religious (especially Christian) doctrine; dissenting, being nonconformist. It only takes on an

evil meaning when sound doctrine is rejected and fallacy is accepted and taught in preference to truth.

14. Envying – pain, ill-will, and jealousy at the good fortune or blessings of another; the most base of all degrading and disgraceful passions.

15. Murders – to kill; to spoil or mar the happiness of another; hatred

Two Sins of Appetite:

16. Drunkenness – intoxicated living; a slave to drink; drinking bouts

17. Revelry – rioting, lascivious and boisterous feastings with obscene music, and other sinful activities; pleasures; carousing

We will all experience temptation because of the innate pleasure of sin. When we are tempted, our Christ-like integrity, the fruit of the Spirit, is at stake. But the one who bare His character will do the right thing even in our secret life.

To counter such works of the flesh, our primary weapons are the invisible weapons of Love and the Fruit of the Holy Spirit we just discussed. When your colleague or family member comes at you with hate and you respond in a gentle and loving way, it completely disarms them. That spirit of hate is silenced and they put down their weapons.

Whether we are being tested or tempted, we must trust that God is refining us. He is busy shaping, remaking and remolding us. He has given us the neck of our enemies – not to be confused with anything of flesh and blood – but those demonic entities that lurk in the dark crevasses of our soul. They do their best work in the darkest hour, but when the enemy thinks he is winning, God is about to pull one over on him. We must resist the enemy and we will walk out of this refined!

Do not turn back from the process as it will only cause a repeat season in your life, specifically, in the area you failed to conquer. Take up your shield of faith, strap on the boots of the gospel of peace, and ride this out, knowing He is uprooting everything that is not of Him. You made it through the crisis, so don't allow the aftermath to take you out. If you can stand to be broken, you can stand to be made whole again. The other side of this will be Glorious!

Trust Him all the way to the end, even if it looks like the only option is decay or death to all areas of concern. Abram did just this when he offered up Isaac, the son of promise. He must have been solely tempted to preserve the life of his precious son and to perpetuate his legacy – however, for the sake of his integrity, he never yielded to it.

It is up to God to bring forth what He has promised in

your life. If He chooses to do it by death or decay, if everything you've built up must come to ruin, trust Him in spite of the loss. It is a test of the heart. Just know, if it dies, He can resurrect it and bring it back to life. Trust that when He does not deliver you from something, He immediately gives you the grace to endure it – which is more than enough. His strength will display as absolute perfection in every area of weakness in your life.

When Paul complained about the thorn in his flesh, God said to him: *"My grace is sufficient for thee: for my strength is made perfect in weakness."*

Paul received this, *"Most gladly therefore will I rather glory in my infirmities, that the power of Christ may rest upon me"* (2 Corinthians 12:9).

Instead of reacting negatively towards suffering, Paul decided that a paradigm shift was required. What he is saying here is, "I gladly make a conscious choice to glory in my infirmities so that the power of Christ may rest upon me. This weakness is worth it if the power of Christ is my mantle."

How do I fight the temptation?

So glad you asked. We are to fight in faith and in right living towards God. We must get back to complete righteousness and Holy living before God, for it is here that we can level up on the devil. Resist the enemy during the day of temptation. And, having done all, Stand. Stand, knowing that the trying of your faith works patience. Patience is having her perfect work in you during this storm and you will come out entirely complete, lacking no good thing.

But sometimes, just the way our own children are with us, we are petulant with God, wanting to wander outside our boundaries. We think that God is keeping us from doing what we want to do, when in reality we don't realize it's His protection. All the while, the enemy is roaming around looking for a likely candidate to devour.

All that God is and does operates out of love and all He wants is our commitment to Him. Therefore, stand firm, for only the ones left standing will see the full salvation of the Lord.

Stand as Job did in the face of all the onslaughts of the enemy. With the loss of his children, his livestock and all his possessions, his health and dignity – his body covered in sores – he was the object of pity and scorn. But he stood his ground and never cursed God in spite of his wife's taunts. He just sat in the ashes in bewilderment, seeking God for an answer (Job 1 and 2).

Now this is important. When the adversary sent Job's self-righteous friends to "comfort" him, they tried to convince him to repent, for surely he had sinned. But Job always maintained his integrity and right-standing with God. You, too, after you have examined yourself and put on the breastplate of righteousness, must resist the attempts of well-meaning people to find fault with you. The matter has been settled between you and God. Don't beat yourself up.

Adversity comes in waves. But just as God has set a limit to the waves on the shore, so has God set limits on how much a person can take. Take comfort from God's assurance in 1 Corinthians 10:13 NLT:

> *The temptations in your life are no different from what others experience. And God is faithful. He will not allow the temptation to be more than you can stand. When you are tempted, he will show you a way out so that you can endure.*

So be comforted that this affliction is only for a moment but it is working towards a far greater eternal weight of glory in your life. We must train ourselves to be aware of the way of escape He has promised to provide to us in each temptation. Prepare the way for others in your sphere of influence so that He may show them His love and protection too.

# THREE CASE
# STUDIES

I n this chapter we will apply what we have learned so far about the armor of God. We will look at two storms, one, storms caused by others and, two, storms that are self-induced. We will close by looking at the paradox of joy in the midst of suffering as we learn to accept storms for Christ.

## STORMS CAUSED BY OTHERS

There are times when we are caught in storms caused by those close to us, who simply want to go contrary to the right path based on their own judgment, experience or skill. This could be a parent, a child, a spouse, a relative, a sibling, friend, boss, co-worker; it could be driven by our economy, a financial or health or relationship crisis. We have no control over this kind of storm because things have already been set in motion. In these moments, we must trust God more than ever in His plan to bring us to a good resolve because His thoughts for us are only for good and not for evil (Jeremiah 29:11).

The case of Paul's storm at sea (Acts 27:9-44)

Paul was sailing as a prisoner together with many other prisoners in a ship bound for Rome for his trial. When they anchored at a safe haven close to Crete, the weather became threatening and Paul advised the centurion not to put out to sea again as it would be treacherous. Nevertheless, the centurion believed the master and owner of the ship more than Paul. The wind subsided, which led them to believe in a peaceful calm; but once they were out again, it quickly turned against them. Now, even though Paul had warned them not to sail, he was not exempt from the direct actions of the men who had made the wrong decision. He was in just as much danger as the other prisoners and crew.

As we read, I would like you to consider the following questions:

Question 1: Who or what do you think caused the storm – nature or the devil? If the latter, what might have been his intention?

Question 2: What strongholds of the enemy might Paul have had to pull down?

Question 3: How much of the full armor of God do you see displayed by Paul in this crisis?

So here we go!

In such a desperate situation, what would you have done had you been Paul? You got it right. Pray and intercede. Seek the Lord. That's exactly what he did. He waited to hear clearly from God, so he could convey these instructions to the centurion and men.

In the pitch darkness, as they drew near the island, they feared that they would hit the rocks and suffer shipwreck. Knowing that some of the sailors intended to jump ship for their own lives, Paul warned the centurion that unless they stayed on board they would not be saved.

Then the soldiers cut off the ropes of the boat, and let her drift. When it was day Paul urged them all to eat, and guaranteed their safety.

*And while the day was coming on, Paul besought them all to take meat, saying, This day is the fourteenth day that ye have tarried and continued fasting, having taken nothing. Wherefore I pray you to take some meat: for this is for your health: for there shall not an hair fall from the head of any of you. And when he had thus spoken, he took bread, and gave thanks to God in presence of them all: and when he had broken it, he began to eat Then were they all of good cheer, and they also took some meat. And we were in all in the ship two hundred threescore and sixteen souls. And when they had eaten enough, they lightened the ship, and cast out the wheat into the sea* (Acts 27:33-38).

These words of comfort and exhortation from God greatly cheered the men and gave them the will to live.

Though the ship ran aground and broke into pieces, all those on board managed to escape holding on to boards and reached the shore in safety. Due to Paul's timely advice and intercession, not a single person perished in the shipwreck (Acts 27:9-44).

Now let's go back to our questions.

Question 1: Who or what do you think caused
the storm – nature or the devil? If the latter,
what might have been his intention?

On the surface it looked like a natural event. Violent
storms in the Mediterranean are common in the winter due
to the strong winds. But look a little closer at the back story
to Paul's trial in Rome. Paul was being charged for disturbing
the peace and inciting violence. He insisted on being tried in
Rome because he was a Roman citizen. Ostensibly, this was
a legal matter but his real motive was kingdom business: to
fulfill God's plan for him to go to Rome and thereby share
the gospel before the highest authorities.

The devil knew this plan and his counter measure was
to obstruct it by any means possible. The sea journey at this
time of the year was the ideal time to stir up the elements to
prevent Paul from reaching Rome. If the devil could cause a
shipwreck, that would be ideal, and if that meant the end of
Paul and all the others on board, that would make his day!

Paul had already warned the master of the ship about the
risk. But the master ignored this advice because he trusted
his expert knowledge over that of a layman –was the stronghold of pride at work here? Moreover, the devil presented a
deceptively calm sea at the time. So from what his eyes saw,
and for the sake of convenience, the master using his human

reasoning; he decided now was the best time to make a break for it and put out to sea.

Question 2: What strongholds of the enemy
might Paul have had to pull down?

We discussed the possible stronghold of pride in the ship's master, which led him to be easily deceived by the stillness of the sea.

What about Paul? Could he have developed strongholds that needed to be pulled down?

Here he was in a situation, where the master of the ship did not heed his prudent advice, and now all of them were in danger of their lives. It also threatened to short-circuit Paul's mission to Rome. Quite justifiably, feelings of rage, hostility, resentment and bitterness could have built up, activating any of the Nine Sins of Temper we read about in chapter 4.

Paul would have to deal with all the thoughts and emotions whirling in his head. He would have to bring them into order and submission to Christ.

Question 3: How much of the full armor of
God do you see displayed in Paul in this crisis?

Paul guarded his heart and mind (breastplate, helmet) and did not allow himself to succumb to resentment or anger at the leaders. Neither did he operate from a mean, vengeful spirit with them because of their rejection of his advice.

No, he waited on God for continuous revelation throughout the voyage, trusting in Him to lead them out of this danger. He knew his goal. So, while everybody was in a state of panic, he was calm and at peace (belt of truth, shield of faith, helmet).

He knew that God would deliver him but he prayed as well for the safety of all 276 men on board. He spoke life-giving words to the men, urging them to eat and be optimistic, for God would surely deliver them from all harm. He broke bread and gave thanks to God in the presence of them all. Seeing his faith and closeness to God, many received hope again, and they would surely have wanted to know about the God he served. Then, when some of the sailors wanted to abandon the ship and swim ashore to save themselves, he warned them there would be no safety except they remain on board, and appealed to their sense of responsibility. All these reflect the weapons of prayer, faith, perseverance, love, gospel shoes, and sword of the spirit.

So what do you do when you find yourself in a storm caused by others?

You guard your heart with all diligence, *"for out of it are the issues of life"* (Proverbs 4:23). You put on faith, you pray and, when you hear from God, you share those words of assurance with those around you to include, in most cases, those who may have caused the storm.

If we walk closely with God, we will know that nothing can separate us from His love and plan for us (Romans 8:38-39). Such a strong sense of security in who God is will change how we go through tough times. Even when storms are foisted upon us by others, we can still trust that all things work together for good for those who love the Lord and who are the called according to His purpose (Romans 8:28).

This kind of a storm will cause us to review our perspective on life and our priorities. None of our accomplishments and goals matter at this moment. It is here the true value of life will surface. It is here the true soldier of God shows his mettle.

# SELF-INDUCED STORMS

Just as others may be the cause of storms in our own life, we ourselves may be the cause of storms in the lives of ourselves and others. This may happen unwittingly when we go about our pursuits without thinking about their effect on others.

Let's look more closely into self-induced storms.

The case of Jonah

Jonah didn't care about anyone when he fled from God. He simply did not want to go to Nineveh to preach repentance to this wicked city and thus save them from God's wrath. So he embarked on a ship bound for Tarshish on the other side of the Mediterranean.

Here were his orders:

*Arise, go to Nineveh, that great city, and cry against it; for their wickedness is come up before me* (Jonah 1:2).

God was sending the prophet to these people with a message of judgment, but Jonah declined. Instead of accepting his assignment to speak on behalf of God, he decided to run as far as he could get.

What may have prompted this move?

The city of Nineveh, founded by Nimrod, was not far from the northern Israel capital, Samaria. Nineveh was then at the height of its prosperity. But it was also noted for its evil and cruel ways to its enemies, and certainly Israel was one of them.

So Jonah may have been afraid of confronting such a fierce people. Very likely as well, Jonah had developed a hatred for these people and, out of unforgiveness and revenge, was determined not to give them the chance to repent. For

God only warns so as to give people time to repent, and if they repent, He is always merciful and withdraws judgment.

Jonah was probably thinking. "I will attempt in my finite capacity to stand against the deliverance of this entire city. If I run away, this deliverance will not happen. I will not be the agent to a city where thousands upon thousands of people who are lost and destitute can be set free."

How did he expect the story to end? The truth is he was so intent on running away, he may not have given any thought to anything or anyone else. We must steer clear of falling into our own plans in defiance of what God has instructed us to do. Are we more concerned about our agendas than about yielding to the will of God?

But the LORD intervened and caused a great tempest in the sea, so that the ship was almost broken. The sailors were afraid and cried out to their gods to save them. Finding Jonah asleep, they entreated on him to call upon his God too.

Then they decided to cast lots to find out who had caused this evil. Jonah was found out. He could hide no longer. So he confessed that he had fled from God, and he revealed his identity, *"I am an Hebrew; and I fear the LORD, the God of heaven, which hath made the sea and the dry land."*

Then he offered himself, *"Take me up, and cast me forth*

*into the sea; so shall the sea be calm unto you: for I know that for my sake this great tempest is upon you.*"

The men tried to avoid this by rowing hard towards the land; but they could not make it because of the rough seas. In desperation, they too cried out to the God of Jonah, "*We beseech thee, O LORD, we beseech thee, let us not perish for this man's life, and lay not upon us innocent blood: for thou, O LORD, hast done as it pleased thee.*"

Finally, they had no choice but to cast Jonah into the sea. When they did, the miraculous happened: the raging of the sea ceased. The men were exceedingly fearful, and offered a sacrifice to the LORD, and made vows to Him.

Jonah had caused great hardship and danger to the lives of these men because of his disobedience, selfishness and prejudice against the people of Nineveh. But, tossed into that raging sea, was Jonah punished? Did he drown? No. God was merciful and was about to reveal Himself to him. He caused a great fish to swallow Jonah up and keep him in its belly for three days and three nights.

When we come to that narrow place between life and death, then the most crucial matters come to the fore.

By now Jonah had come to the end of himself and here is where the change of heart (repentance) took place. Hear his cry to God from that dark dank place:

*Then Jonah prayed unto the* Lord *his God out of the fish's belly,*

*And said, I cried by reason of mine affliction unto the* Lord, *and he heard me; out of the belly of hell cried I, and thou heardest my voice. For thou hadst cast me into the deep, in the midst of the seas; and the floods compassed me about: all thy billows and thy waves passed over me.*

*Then I said, I am cast out of thy sight; yet I will look again toward thy holy temple. The waters compassed me about, even to the soul: the depth closed me round about, the weeds were wrapped about my head.*

*I went down to the bottoms of the mountains; the earth with her bars was about me for ever: yet hast thou brought up my life from corruption, O* Lord *my God. When my soul fainted within me I remembered the* Lord: *and my prayer came in unto thee, into thine holy temple. They that observe lying vanities forsake their own mercy. But I will sacrifice unto thee with the voice of thanksgiving; I will pay that that I have vowed. Salvation is of the* Lord.

*And the LORD spake unto the fish, and it vomited
out Jonah upon the dry land* (Jonah 2:1-10).

The Lord had delivered Jonah and He now came to him
a second time with the same proposition:

*Arise, go unto Nineveh, that great city, and
preach unto it the preaching that I bid thee.*

This time there was no argument.

*So Jonah arose, and went unto Nineveh, accord-
ing to the word of the LORD. Now Nineveh was
an exceeding great city of three days' journey.
And Jonah began to enter into the city a day's
journey, and he cried, and said, Yet forty days,
and Nineveh shall be overthrown.*

*So the people of Nineveh believed God, and pro-
claimed a fast, and put on sackcloth, from the
greatest of them even to the least of them. For
word came unto the king of Nineveh, and he
arose from his throne, and he laid his robe from
him, and covered him with sackcloth, and sat
in ashes.*

*And he caused it to be proclaimed and published*
*through Nineveh by the decree of the king and*
*his nobles, saying, Let neither man nor beast,*
*herd nor flock, taste any thing: let them not feed,*
*nor drink water: But let man and beast be cov-*
*ered with sackcloth, and cry mightily unto God:*
*yea, let them turn every one from his evil way,*
*and from the violence that is in their hands.*

*Who can tell if God will turn and repent, and*
*turn away from his fierce anger, that we per-*
*ish not?*

*And God saw their works, that they turned from*
*their evil way; and God repented of the evil, that*
*he had said that he would do unto them; and he*
*did it not* (Jonah 3:2-10).

What a wonderful picture of salvation! The whole city
coming to God in sackcloth and fasting led by the king
himself. It was genuine repentance because it says, *"God saw*
*their works, that they turned from their evil way"* (verse 10) and
He relented from judgment.

This whole episode demonstrates the goodness and mercy
of God at so many levels. First, at the level of Jonah's ship
mates. Although they were idol worshipers, they began to see

that Yahweh, the mighty and sovereign God controlled all the elements, and they turned their prayer from their worthless idols to Him. Even when we take off our gospel shoes, God is still at work, giving all those in our sphere of influence the opportunity to hear the good news. He can turn around bad for good. So, even if Jonah's carelessness put their lives at risk, through him they came to know the one, true and living God and His goodness to them.

What is also amazing is that the people of Nineveh were moved to deep repentance. The entire city was transformed. I do not know how long and how eloquently Jonah preached but I know that his testimony spoke more eloquently than his words. After that storm and encounter with God in the belly of the whale, Jonah had a story to tell that would melt the hearts of the most hardened.

And as for Jonah, God did not forsake him in spite of his rebellion. He did not simply assign someone else to do the job but He gave him a chance to really understand His nature. In that brief period, God was doing a deep work of changing Jonah's heart from one of hatred and vengeance to one of compassion. Truly, the goodness of God leads us to repentance (Romans 2:4). And rather than strip him of his ministry, God anointed him afresh through his trial by water!

# Going though Storms
# for Christ

This leads us to consider the sufferings we go through for Christ's sake. Let us look at Paul again.

Even before the outset Paul's missionary journey, he was singled out as one destined for suffering for the sake of Christ. This was the word the disciple Ananias received from the Lord when Saul was struck down with blindness on the road to Damascus. At the time, Saul had no clue what was happening to him or the magnitude of the calling of God.

> *Then Ananias answered, Lord, I have heard by many of this man, how much evil he hath done to thy saints at Jerusalem: And here he hath authority from the chief priests to bind all that call on thy name.*

> *But the Lord said unto him, Go thy way: for he is a chosen vessel unto me, to bear my name before the Gentiles, and kings, and the children of Israel: For I will shew him great things **he must suffer for my name's sake** (Acts 9:10-16, emphasis added).*

This is a very prophetic word, for Paul did indeed suffer

many hardships for the sake of the gospel. But these were overshadowed by great and mighty victories as the gospel penetrated the region. Finally, Paul was told to go to back to Jerusalem, not knowing what would befall him there, but mindful of the intents of the religious elite. However, he was not moved but secure in this one thing: he counted his life as no longer dear to him, and set his mind on finishing his course with joy.

> *And now, behold, I go bound in the spirit unto Jerusalem, not knowing the things that shall befall me there: Save that the Holy Ghost witnesseth in every city, saying that bonds and afflictions abide me.*
>
> *But none of these things move me, neither count I my life dear unto myself, so that I might finish my course with joy, and the ministry, which I have received of the Lord Jesus, to testify the gospel of the grace of God. And now, behold, I know that ye all, among whom I have gone preaching the kingdom of God, shall see my face no more* (Acts 20:22-25).

He had given his life over to the Lord to suffer for Him.

This is what you call a life poured out unto the Lord. This was cause for joy.

> *But even if I am being poured out as a drink offering on the sacrifice and service of your faith, I am glad and rejoice with you all* (Philippians 2:17).

This reminds us of Jesus' words about the value of losing our soul life.

> *He that findeth his life shall lose it: and he that loseth **his life** for my sake shall find it … For whosoever will save **his life** shall lose it: and whosoever will lose his life for my sake shall find it* (Matthew 10:39, 16:13, emphasis added).

In the above scriptures, the Greek word Jesus uses for "life" is the word *psuche,* which denotes the life of our soul – that of our mind and emotions. Jesus is saying, "Beloved, do not hold on to the life of the self, and be absorbed in your individual pursuits. Do not be governed by your own thoughts and dictated to by your emotions. But give them over to the heart of God – even die to them – that you may experience the abundant life I have for you."

That is how Paul at the end of his life, faced with prison, a trial, and possible execution, could say:

*Brethren, I count not myself to have appre-hended: but this one thing I do, forgetting those things which are behind, and reaching forth unto those things which are before, I press to-ward the mark for the prize of the high calling of God in Christ Jesus* ... (Philippians 3:13-14)

*That I may know him, and the power of his resurrection, and the fellowship of his suf-ferings, being made conformable unto his death* ...(Philippians 3:10)

Are you ready to surrender your self-life?

# A PERSONAL
# CALL TO ARMS

ear reader, you may be going through storms in
your life and it is my prayer that this book has
helped you. I would like to share from the heart
something of the storm I too went through and how the Lord
taught me to overcome.

The last season of my life was a very dark time for me. I
found myself questioning everything I knew and saw about
God. The protracted storm that hit me rocked me to the
core, and I felt at any moment I could totally lose my mind.
But God kept me. He caused me to search for Him in a new
way. It meant a radical shift in my understanding of my faith,

which caused me to challenge all that I had experienced in church and in my Christian belief system as a whole.

You see, it was a storm that neither religion nor tradition could save me from. No, it was only God I desperately needed. Only His supernatural power could deliver me from my fears and bring me peace in the midst of turmoil. I had no more crutches of church and religion to hold on to. There was just me, God and Satan. I chose to cling to God and abandon everything that was in the way – and that included my mindset. My dire straits challenged me to be completely honest with myself and search within myself what I truly believed about God and His Word, His plan for my life and His love for me.

Looking back, I had grown up where I saw the true signs and miracles of God on display. I saw blind eyes open, cataracts fall from eyes, the deaf hear, the dumb speak, the lame get out of wheel chairs, and walk, highly intoxicated people would stagger and stumble in and leave out completely sober, the alters would flood each night with souls ready to surrender their lives to Jesus. During those miraculous times, I even saw my dad live a consecrated life, where he fasted, prayed, and wholeheartedly sought God. And God used Him mightily for His Glory.

However, as I grew older, I moved away from the church,

so to speak – though in my heart I had never left God. I had seen so much hurt and disappointment in the church and I associated it with God. Like Jonah, trying to run away from his calling, I got into modeling and married a professional football player. I remember thinking when I met him for the first time, that he would be the one to get me as far away as I could possibly go.

My journey back to seeking God began in 2016 where I gave my life to Him in total surrender to His will. I decided that I would give up everything for Him so I could fulfill my purpose, the one God had designed for me. In 2017, I resigned from my job and relocated to a different state in the hope of receiving love and security from my family. I will never forget the day I left – March 29, 2017. There was a horrendous storm. I remember asking God if I should turn back and He responded, "No, the principalities have bestirred themselves against you." I could not understand how or why but I was on this journey with God. I spent a year there, and then relocated.

Seeking acceptance and love has cost me a great deal. I had no idea that God had called me out and set me apart. He made me different on purpose, although initially I thought there was something wrong with me because I did not fit the usual mold, not even with family. But then I came to realize it was all by design.

By 2018 my soul had landed in a hell-on-earth experience. This led me to a church, where a Prophetess spoke this word over my life: "The Lord told me that He had sent you here and that I see happiness around you. There is an event that will take place in your life that will bring you great happiness. God brought you here because there is a place you have to get to in the Spirit."

I interpreted the promise in the order it was given, not realizing that God often tells us the end before the beginning. I spent a long while searching for that happiness He promised but instead found myself going through great hardship. At the back of my mind there was this place I had to get to in the Spirit. However, I saw nothing close to happiness, not a single thing resembling it.

So, I began to question God about His Word and His promise to me. It was then I realized He often shows us the end before the beginning. It was absolutely my fault that I did not understand how He operates. I knew the onus was now on me to get outside of myself and be willing to accept His timing, not my own, and to recognize what He was doing in my life.

I will admit that the promise of happiness kept me

holding on to fight and not to give up on Him. I knew that somehow I had to get to this unknown place. Everything in my life – my survival and my faith – hinged on this promise. I had to allow God to do a complete overhaul of me from the inside out. My outward life that appeared to be so glamorous was just tinsel, hiding my brokenness, hardship and despair. People looked at me and thought, "Wow, she has everything!" But, in reality I had nothing. Little did they know the turmoil, hurt and pain in my inner life.

It was not until I began to truly seek His face during this dark season that I came to discover the truth of who He is and how much He truly loves me. I had to examine my belief system to find out what I held as the truth concerning Him. This meant completely abandoning what I experienced in church. I needed more – something real and authentic. I knew this would cost me everything but I had nothing to lose in the living hell that had become my reality. Only God knows the depth of the evil that afflicted my soul. So it was necessary to go back to boot camp to seek the face of God with all of my heart, mind and soul, asking for His will and way, no longer my own. I knew it would cost me everything I deemed Tabitha to be; but, considering what I was facing, I had no choice.

To help me become secure in that mold which is His, He

affirmed me. He called me, and assured me He has approved me and sealed me for His purpose. The truth that I began to discover about Him is the reason for writing this series of books. I want to let others know He is real, and to encourage them never to give up on Him.

Each book then is a testimony of my life. *Enriching the Immortal Soul* was written because I had to find the right path to Him, and this is the one He gave me. I had to adopt a lifestyle emptied out in obedience to Him. *Understanding God's plan* is based on a dream of two men in different places in life but with the same journeys end an absolute surrender.

*Purpose for Pain* was written after inquiring of the Lord because I had to go through the intense pain and suffering. His response was: "There were keys that you needed and not just you – others need them too." I asked how I was to let others know and how I could I locate all of them. He replied, "I want you to write them and put them in a book." All of the books He directed are essential keys that are needed in the lives of believers.

The present book *Weathering Life's Storms* is to reveal the true enemy in life and our weapons to defeat him so that we can stop destroying one another especially as Christians – our families, our marriages, our children and all the people we love.

He has invested more than we will ever know, and He always gets the return on His investment. So, no matter what happens in life, He will come through because His word is at stake. He will not fail as failure is impossible with Him. He is sovereign and all-knowing: He knows the past, the present and the future in one glance. It takes a while for us to see the whole picture clearly but He is not bound by time. He sees both the end and the beginning at once.

We have to come to a place of maturity to recognize who our true enemy is and the tactics he is using against us. We need to understand that God requires more of us – and that is right and holy living. We must be willing to pay the price of walking in the wisdom and authority given to us, and that requires that we see ourselves as trustworthy.

In this discovery I learned that I would have to take this journey into my past with Him, and that meant revisiting all the places of pain, rejection and betrayal in my life. He would allow me to experience each place of fear and damage so that I could be healed and delivered from the things that were hiding in the dark crevices of my soul. For it is only in that place of pain that true forgiveness *from the heart* can be extended to the offender (Matthew 18:35). This was a costly lesson for me, but it was necessary to let Him hold my hand through all those places of hurt and destruction.

It was there that I could forgive with His compassion, and from there receive His deliverance, wholeness and freedom. This helped me to forgive others completely from my heart and in each season of suffering and hardship caused by the human hand. I had to let Him be Lord over every demoralized area in my life. I had to learn that His love for me is not like any human love I have experienced.

He gave me another word and told me that I would see a return on my investment. I held on to this word as if my life depended upon it, and it did come to fruition. All I had to do was hold on to the promise that He gave me; that was enough to keep me fighting. In the process I came to trust in Him as a Person who keeps His word. I knew He would watch over it to perform it according to what it was sent out to do. So, I took it as my responsibility to stand in faith everyday for as long as it took. I made sure I surrendered my new self to Him and died to the old Tabitha each day.

To learn and grow in His unconditional love means you will sometimes be put in situations where you have to love the unlovable or those with stones in their heart. It would involve loving them in spite of their weaknesses and faults, even when they damage your heart. When you allow the love of God to flow through you, you can say in the moment of hurt and despair, "I love you and I forgive you."

When that happens, you can truly bless people who actually speak curses on you. Bless them and remain loving even if they are the ones closest to you who can say, "I love you," in one breath and then turn around and betray you. It is not until you can walk in love and forgiveness from your heart that your heart life will be pleasing to the Lord. When you are exposed to their deeds firsthand and yet choose to love, then you have won a great victory.

And so, my brothers and sisters, you can see it is in all this turbulence that I have learned to put on the full armor of God. I had to put on my helmet of salvation and shield of faith and learn to let Him carry me. I had to trust that He would put no more burdens on me than I was capable of bearing and, if He allowed them, then I could endure them in His strength. When I put on the belt of truth, I was ready to accept the fact of life that it is often the people closest to you that are capable of betraying you. That was a stabbing pain but I could live with it because I knew that God wanted to heal my deepest wounds. And as I forgave, I would also raise the sword of the Spirit and speak life-giving words over the offender. I learned to pull down the stronghold of deception – that false belief system I'd formed of Him – a human fabrication of God that I had created in my mind, fashioned in the likeness of man.

The great thing is that the more I began to seek Him, the more I found out about Him – His ways and His nature. And, like Job when he uttered, "I had heard of you but this day with my own eyes have I seen you. I now have my own revelation of who you are because of this," I was beginning to discover a new dimension of my God.

When we see Him as He really is, only then are we prepared to be like Him. We must put on the nature of Christ so that when the enemy sees us, he sees Christ. When we have on Christ's breastplate, we are hidden in Him. We must put on the fruit of the Spirit, which fortify us against temptation to our fleshly desires and nature. We weather the storms of life because we know that in them our faith will be tried and in patience we will possess our souls. We will be made whole and complete in Him with no good thing lacking because we now have His desires, nature and character within us.

There is a great price to pay for the anointing and power of God. The question is: are we willing to pay the price in the denial of self to receive the outpouring? The enemy constantly tries to bait us with the lure of worldly ambitions so that we lose our resolve to give up all for God. Are we willing to stand in humility when pride rears its head? Are we willing to abstain when an invitation is put out to satisfy the flesh? Will we commit to rejecting fear and putting on the boldness of Christ? Then we are truly sons of God fully armed for the day of battle.

# References

Chapter 2

*Dake Annotated Reference Bible*, Finis Jennings Dake, Dake Publishing, (1963)

*God's Plan for Man, Finis Jennings Dake, Dake Publishing, (1949)*

**Books by Tabitha Henton Lamb**


Understanding God's Plan

Re-evaluating Your Relationship With God


The Purpose of Pain

How God Uses Pain to Strengthen Your Resolve


Enriching the Immortal Soul

A Journey Towards God


*Available whereever books are sold.*